THE POETRY OF TECHNETIUM

The Poetry of Technetium

Walter the Educator

SKB

Silent King Books a WhichHead imprint

Copyright © 2023 by Walter the Educator

All rights reserved. No part of this book may be reproduced in any manner whatsoever without written permission except in the case of brief quotations embodied in critical articles and reviews.

First Printing, 2023

Disclaimer
This book is a literary work; poems are not about specific persons, locations, situations, and/or circumstances unless mentioned in a historical context. This book is for entertainment and informational purposes only. The author and publisher offer this information without warranties expressed or implied. No matter the grounds, neither the author nor the publisher will be accountable for any losses, injuries, or other damages caused by the reader's use of this book. The use of this book acknowledges an understanding and acceptance of this disclaimer.

"Earning a degree in chemistry changed my life!"
— Walter the Educator

dedicated to all the chemistry lovers, like myself, across the world

CONTENTS

Dedication v

Why I Created This Book? 1

One - 43 2

Two - Symbol Of Hope 4

Three - Possibility Gleams 6

Four - Shall Never End 8

Five - Forever Resolute 10

Six - Testament To Science 12

Seven - Dear Technetium 14

Eight - Possibilities Flee 16

Nine - Brighter Day 18

Ten - Leads Us Through 20

Eleven - Silent Hero 22

Twelve - A Marvel 24

Thirteen - Catalyst Of Discovery	. . . . . .	26
Fourteen - Beacon Of Chemistry	. . . . . .	28
Fifteen - Technetium-99m	. . . . . .	30
Sixteen - Infinite Flair	. . . . . .	32
Seventeen - Element We Respect	. . . . . .	34
Eighteen - Joy And Cheer	. . . .	36
Nineteen - No North	. . . .	38
Twenty - Incredible Power	. . . . . .	40
Twenty-One - Forever True	. . . . . .	42
Twenty-Two - Science We Proclaim	. . . . .	44
Twenty-Three - Cosmic Bazaars	. . . . . .	46
Twenty-Four - Wonders Of Eternity	. . . . .	48
Twenty-Five - Unlocking The Future	. . . . .	50
Twenty-Six - Annals Of Space	. . . . . .	52
Twenty-Seven - Enlightening Our Minds	. . . .	54
Twenty-Eight - Curiosity's Arc	. . . . . .	56
Twenty-Nine - Pioneer Of Progress	. . . . .	58
Thirty - Abundant And Strong	. . . .	60
Thirty-One - Endless Delight	. . . .	62
Thirty-Two - Higher And Higher	. . . . . .	64

Thirty-Three - Inspire And Guide 66

Thirty-Four - Creator Of Art 68

Thirty-Five - Technetium, Element Of Mystery 70

About The Author 72

WHY I CREATED THIS BOOK?

Creating a poetry book about the chemical element of Technetium was a unique and fascinating endeavor. Technetium is an intriguing element in the periodic table as it is the first element to be artificially produced. It has various applications in nuclear medicine and research. By exploring the characteristics and properties of Technetium through poetry, I can delve into its scientific significance, historical context, and symbolic representations. This approach allows for a creative fusion of science and art, bringing together the worlds of chemistry and poetry. It can also serve as a means to educate and engage readers in a different way, making science more accessible and relatable.

ONE

43

In a realm of elements, mysterious and rare,
Lies Technetium, beyond compare.
Atomic number 43, its identity bright,
A shining star in the periodic light.

Born in stellar furnaces, where stars ignite,
Technetium emerges, a celestial sight.
A fleeting existence, a cosmic dance,
It captures our curiosity, a scientific trance.

Unstable and elusive, a radioactive soul,
Technetium's presence takes a heavy toll.
With electrons in disarray, it seeks stability,
A yearning for balance, a quest for tranquility.

In labs and reactors, scientists strive,
To harness its power, to help us survive.

From medicine to industry, its potential untold,
Technetium's secrets, waiting to unfold.

A beacon of innovation, a promise of hope,
Technetium illuminates the path we grope.
In imaging and diagnosis, it plays a vital role,
Guiding the way to healing, making us whole.

Oh Technetium, element of wonder,
You inspire our minds as we ponder.
Your enigmatic nature, a scientific delight,
Forever captivating, shining so bright.

So let us explore, unravel your mystery,
To embrace your essence, in all its glory.
Technetium, a symbol of human ambition,
A testament to our limitless vision.

TWO

SYMBOL OF HOPE

In the realm of elements rare and bright,
There lies a mystery, a captivating light.
Technetium, a name whispered with awe,
A cosmic child born in stellar furnace' maw.

Radiant and fleeting, a radioactive dance,
Its atoms pulsate in a cosmic expanse.
From nuclear fusion, its journey begins,
A fleeting existence, where chaos and beauty spins.

Oh, Technetium, a beacon of innovation,
Guiding us towards healing's transformation.
In medicine's realm, you hold a key,
A tracer in veins, revealing life's mystery.

Industry beckons, with promises untold,
Your power, Technetium, a treasure to behold.
In nuclear reactors, your energy's release,
A source of power that brings the world peace.

Yet, your presence is scarce, your touch is rare,
A symbol of ambition, a vision we share.
Technetium, you inspire us to reach for the sky,
To explore the unknown, where wonders lie.

With boundless potential, you ignite our desire,
To unravel the secrets, to quench our thirst for fire.
Oh, Technetium, element of dreams untold,
In your ethereal essence, our stories unfold.

So, let us embrace you, Technetium divine,
As we journey together, our futures entwined.
For in your atomic structure, we find a spark,
A symbol of hope, a light in the dark.

THREE

POSSIBILITY GLEAMS

In the depths of the periodic table's maze,
Lies a treasure, scarce and rare,
Technetium, a metal that amazes,
With its atomic number, a secret to share.

Hidden amidst the elements, it resides,
A shimmering enigma, waiting to be found,
A creation of nature, a mystery that guides,
The curious minds, forever spellbound.

In medicine's realm, it finds its place,
A beacon of hope, a diagnostic grace,
Radiopharmaceuticals, its healing embrace,
Unveiling the secrets of life's intricate maze.

In industry, it dances with grace,
A catalyst, igniting progress with its flame,

Transforming reactions, a champion of space,
Advancing technology, forever in its name.
 Oh Technetium, elusive and grand,
A symbol of innovation, forever in demand,
Your fleeting nature, a marvel to behold,
A testament to human ambition, untold.
 So let us celebrate your mysteries untamed,
With awe and wonder, forever inflamed,
Technetium, the element of dreams,
A symbol of hope, where possibility gleams.

FOUR

SHALL NEVER END

In the depths of the periodic realm,
Where secrets of atoms overwhelm,
Lies a treasure, rare and grand,
A captivating element, you must understand.

Technetium, a name unknown,
A symphony of protons, all alone,
In the vast expanse of periodicity,
It shines with an elusive rarity.

In medicine's embrace, it finds its worth,
A healer of bodies, a savior's birth,
Radiopharmaceuticals dance in its wake,
Diagnosing ailments, for life's sake.

In industry's grasp, it fuels the fire,
An innovator's dream, a burning desire,

Catalysts and sensors, it does create,
Pushing boundaries, defying fate.

Yet, it remains a mystery untold,
A story of atoms, yet to unfold,
With half-lives fleeting, it drifts away,
Leaving scientists in a state of dismay.

Technetium, a symbol of human ambition,
A testament to our relentless mission,
To unravel the secrets of the unknown,
And carve a path to a future yet to be shown.

So let us marvel at this element divine,
A spark of potential, a treasure to find,
Technetium, oh rare and elusive friend,
In your mysteries, our journey shall never end.

FIVE

FOREVER RESOLUTE

In the depths of the periodic table's realm,
An enigma emerges, Technetium its name.
A fleeting existence, a shimmering gleam,
A dance of electrons, a transient dream.

Born in the heart of stellar fire,
Forged in the cosmic crucible's pyre.
A child of supernovae, a celestial birth,
Technetium emerges, the rarest on earth.

In labs it is sought, a prize to be won,
For its uses in medicine, industry, and beyond.
A tracer in veins, a diagnostic tool,
Revealing secrets hidden, a medical jewel.

In turbines it spins, a catalyst's might,
Enhancing reactions, speeding up flight.

In nuclear power, its power unveiled,
A fuel of the future, its potential unassailed.
   Yet its scarcity intrigues, a mystery untold,
A symbol of ambition, of stories yet unfold.
Technetium, elusive, a challenge to find,
A testament to the human mind.
   In its atomic dance, it beckons us still,
To unravel its secrets, to seek and fulfill.
A symbol of progress, of endless pursuit,
Technetium, the element, forever resolute.

SIX

TESTAMENT TO SCIENCE

In the realm of atoms, a wondrous tale unfolds,
Of an element rare, its secrets yet untold.
Technetium, the enigma, with mysteries to impart,
A jewel of science, a masterpiece of art.

In medicine's embrace, it finds its noblest role,
A beacon of hope, a savior for the soul.
Radiopharmaceuticals, its gift to humanity,
Diagnosing ailments, healing with clarity.

In industry's domain, its power reigns supreme,
A catalyst of progress, a visionary's dream.
Transforming molecules, unlocking nature's code,
Advancing technology, with every episode.

Technetium, a phantom, elusive in its grasp,
Born in supernovae's fiery clasp.

A cosmic dance, in the heavens it did ignite,
Creating stardust, forging Technetium's light.
From lab to lab, its atoms seek their place,
A testament to science's relentless chase.
In the depths of laboratories, where wonders are found,
Technetium's allure, forever unbound.
A symbol of innovation, a symbol of might,
Technetium, a shimmering prism of light.
From medicine to industry, its powers unfold,
A testament to science, a story yet untold.

SEVEN

DEAR TECHNETIUM

In the realm of medicine, a marvel unveiled,
Lies a shimmering element, Technetium unveiled.
A beacon of hope, a healer of pain,
It dances with atoms, a medical gain.

Radiation's ally, a diagnostic charm,
Technetium's touch, a medical alarm.
Injected with care, it navigates through,
Unveiling the secrets, hidden from view.

In hospital halls, its presence is felt,
A silent assistant, where science has dwelt.
From scans on the screen, to images clear,
Technetium whispers, there's nothing to fear.

Beyond the confines of hospitals' walls,
Technetium's power in industry calls.

In nuclear reactors, it quietly thrives,
A catalyst, forging energy's drive.

    Oh, Technetium, element divine,
Your presence, a gift, so rare to find.
A symbol of progress, a beacon of light,
Guiding humanity through the darkest of night.

    Though scarce and elusive, you captivate,
A puzzle to solve, a mystery to relate.
Yet, in your essence, a promise does dwell,
Of innovation and progress, forever to tell.

    Technetium, forever you'll be,
An emblem of human ambition, we'll see.
In medicine, industry, and beyond,
Your potential, dear Technetium, forever we bond.

EIGHT

POSSIBILITIES FLEE

In the depths of science's realm,
A hidden gem, a sacred helm,
Technetium, the enigma of all,
A shimmering star, both big and small.

In medicine's grasp, it finds its way,
A beacon of hope, a light of day,
Radiopharmaceuticals, healing's guide,
Through veins and bones, it does abide.

In industry's embrace, it takes its stand,
A catalyst of progress, a helping hand,
From catalytic converters to oil refining,
Technetium's touch, forever defining.

But beyond these realms, its allure does grow,
A symbol of ambition, a human's shadow,

For in its rarity, a challenge lies,
To harness its power, the dream that flies.
   From lab to lab, the quest unfolds,
To capture the essence, its secrets untold,
Technetium, the puzzle unsolved,
A testament to human resolve.
   So let us marvel at this element's might,
Its many facets shining bright,
For in its presence, we find a spark,
Igniting innovation, leaving a mark.
   Technetium, the enigmatic prize,
A symbol of progress, reaching the skies,
In science's hands, it holds the key,
To a future where infinite possibilities flee.

NINE

BRIGHTER DAY

In the realm of science, a mystery unveiled,
A wondrous element, Technetium hailed.
With atomic number 43, it takes its place,
A catalyst of progress, a symbol of grace.

In the depths of the lab, its secrets unfurled,
Technetium dances, a rare and precious world.
Its isotopes abound, elusive and bright,
Unlocking the mysteries hidden from sight.

Through its power, we gain a diagnostic view,
A beacon of hope, a medical breakthrough.
From the heart to the bones, its radiance gleams,
Revealing the truth, dispelling our dreams.

In industry's embrace, Technetium shines,
Fueling our ambitions with nuclear design.
A power untamed, potential untold,
Unleashing the future, a brilliance foretold.

Yet scarce in its presence, it's a treasure untamed,
A reminder of limits, of dreams unrestrained.
With every discovery, its allure remains,
A symbol of progress, where innovation gains.

Oh Technetium, element so grand,
A catalyst of change, in our human hand.
From medicine to power, you pave the way,
Guiding our journey, to a brighter day.

TEN

LEADS US THROUGH

In labs unseen, where atoms dance,
A gleaming element, Technetium by chance.
Born in stars, a cosmic birth,
Unveiling secrets of the Earth.

In medicine's realm, it takes its place,
A tracer of life, a beacon of grace.
Through veins it flows, a shimmering light,
Guiding doctors, in the darkest of night.

In industry's realm, it finds its niche,
A catalyst of progress, a wizard's pitch.
Unleashing power, with every reaction,
Transforming dreams into solid satisfaction.

In labs and factories, its presence profound,
Transforming elements, with a silent sound.
A metal so rare, a mystery untold,
A fleeting glimpse of the stories it holds.

Technetium, oh element divine,
Symbol of hope, in the grand design.
Unraveling the secrets of the unknown,
A catalyst for progress, till the seeds are sown.
　　So let us marvel at Technetium's might,
A symbol of human ambition and light.
In every discovery, a step towards the new,
Technetium, the element that leads us through.

ELEVEN

SILENT HERO

In the realm of industry, Technetium reigns,
A catalyst of power, it truly sustains.
With its atomic number of forty-three,
It holds the key to a brighter energy.

From nuclear reactors to medical scans,
Technetium shines with its healing plans.
Radiopharmaceuticals, a gift it bestows,
Guiding us through ailments, with precision it knows.

Rare and elusive, this element stands,
Challenging scientists with its untapped demands.
In laboratories, they toil and strive,
Harnessing its potential, trying to derive.

A symbol of progress, innovation's embrace,
Technetium paves the way for a new space.

With its unique properties, it leads the fight,
For breakthroughs and discoveries, day and night.
   Oh Technetium, element of wonder and might,
You illuminate our world, shining so bright.
In industry and medicine, you leave your mark,
A silent hero, lighting up the dark.

TWELVE

A MARVEL

In the realm of elements, a jewel we find,
Technetium, rare and one of a kind.
A metal mysterious, with power untold,
In industry's grasp, its secrets unfold.

In laboratories, its brilliance shines,
A catalyst for progress, a gift divine.
From steel to fuel cells, it lends its might,
Transforming the world with its radiant light.

In reactors it dances, a vibrant display,
Generating energy, day after day.
Nuclear power, a promise it brings,
A clean, boundless source, where hope takes its wings.

From skyscrapers soaring high in the air,
To the machines that drive us everywhere,

Technetium's touch, a mark of its grace,
Unleashing innovation, at an incredible pace.

But beyond industry's grasp, it finds its way,
Into the realm of medicine, where it holds sway.
A beacon of hope, in the fight against ill,
Guiding us through ailments, with a steadfast will.

In imaging scans, it reveals the unseen,
Diagnosing diseases, where answers convene.
A tracer of truth, through the body it flows,
Unveiling mysteries that only it knows.

Technetium, a marvel, a force to behold,
In industry's clasp, or in medical molds.
A catalyst for progress, a healer's guide,
In its atomic embrace, let us confide.

THIRTEEN

CATALYST OF DISCOVERY

In the realm of elements, one stands apart,
A silent hero, a beacon of hope,
Technetium, a catalyst for progress,
Guiding us through the dark, with a radiant scope.

Within the realm of medicine it dwells,
A healer in the form of radiopharmaceuticals,
Imaging scans, a window to our health,
Technetium, the key to diagnostic miracles.

With magic unseen, it dances with ease,
Elusive and rare, its essence untamed,
Challenging scientists to unlock its secrets,
To harness its power, yet never be tamed.

Its properties unique, a marvel untold,
Shimmering hues, a symphony of light,

Technetium, the artist of the elements,
Painting a canvas with colors so bright.

Oh Technetium, you illuminate the world,
Leaving a mark in both industry and medicine,
A silent hero, silently leading the way,
A symbol of hope, forever unbroken.

So let us celebrate this mysterious element,
A gift from the universe, a treasure untold,
Technetium, the catalyst of discovery,
A symbol of progress, forever bold.

FOURTEEN

BEACON OF CHEMISTRY

In realms of science, a marvel resides,
A beacon of progress, where knowledge abides.
Technetium, an element of might,
Guides us through ailments, shining so bright.

Born from the minds of visionaries bold,
Perrier and Segrè, their story untold.
Mendeleev's prophecy, a truth unveiled,
Ekamanganese's secrets finally revealed.

Radiant and rare, Technetium's grace,
In medicine's embrace, it finds its place.
Imaging procedures, its power untold,
Aiding diagnosis, a story unfold.

Man-made yet natural, a paradox rare,
In uranium ore, it finds its lair.

Silvery gray, a transition it claims,
Between manganese and rhenium's flames.
    Isotopes, all radioactive, they gleam,
In red giants, Technetium's dream.
Stars unveil their secrets, elements grand,
Technetium's legacy, forever will stand.
    Symbol of progress, catalyst for discovery,
Technetium, a beacon of chemistry.
Through science's lens, we unravel its lore,
A testament to mankind's quest for more.

FIFTEEN

TECHNETIUM-99M

In the realm of atoms, a mystery lies,
A shimmering element that defies,
Technetium, a name so rare,
In the depths of science, it takes us there.
    Radiopharmaceuticals, its healing art,
A beacon of hope, a brand-new start,
Injected into veins, it courses through,
Illuminating bodies, revealing what's true.
    Technetium-99m, its isotopic might,
In medical imaging, a guiding light,
Through gamma rays, it paints the way,
Diagnosing diseases, night and day.
    From bone scans to heart tests, it lends a hand,
A silent warrior, a medical command,

An element so precious, a gift bestowed,
For every patient, a medical ode.

In labs it's crafted, with skill and care,
A substance so vital, beyond compare,
Technetium, the catalyst for health,
A testament to science's stealth.

So let us celebrate this element grand,
In industry and medicine, it takes a stand,
Technetium, a symbol of progress and more,
Unveiling secrets, unlocking doors.

SIXTEEN

INFINITE FLAIR

In the realm of elements, a gem does reside,
A radiant presence, Technetium its name,
With healing powers, it shines far and wide,
A beacon of hope, in the world of the same.

From ancient stars, this element was born,
In cosmic crucibles, its atoms took form,
A gift from the heavens, to heal and transform,
Technetium, the element of life's norm.

Within its core, a magic resides,
Radiopharmaceuticals, its wondrous creation,
Aiding doctors in their healing strides,
Guiding them to the source of salvation.

Through gamma rays, it seeks out the ill,
Illuminating hidden truths, with precision and skill,

Aiding in diagnosis, with a potent will,
Technetium, the element, a medical thrill.

From industry to medicine, it finds its place,
An element of wonder, in the human race,
Science and discovery, it continues to embrace,
Technetium, the element, in life's grand chase.

So let us admire this element rare,
Technetium, a symbol of hope in the air,
A catalyst for progress, beyond compare,
A testament to science's infinite flair.

SEVENTEEN

ELEMENT WE RESPECT

In the realm of elements, a treasure I've found,
A radiant metal that astounds,
Technetium, a marvel of science and art,
A catalyst for progress, a beacon of our start.

In labs it is born, with atomic might,
An element rare, shining so bright,
Unveiling secrets, hidden from sight,
Technetium, the element of purest light.

In medicine's realm, it plays a key role,
Guiding doctors in their healing stroll,
A tracer of hope, a diagnostic aid,
Revealing truths, a path that's laid.

Through gamma rays, it illuminates,
Unveiling mysteries, unlocking the gates,

Within our bodies, it seeks its way,
Technetium, leading us closer each day.

In industry's grasp, it finds its due,
Aiding in progress, innovation anew,
From nuclear reactors, to cutting-edge tech,
Technetium, the element we respect.

Oh Technetium, in you we find,
A symbol of science's infinite mind,
A testament to human endeavor,
Forever we'll cherish you, now and forever.

EIGHTEEN

JOY AND CHEER

In the realm of atoms, a shining star,
Technetium, the element bizarre.
A beacon of science, a radiant light,
Unveiling secrets, in the darkest night.

With atomic number 43 it stands,
A marvel of nature, in scientific hands.
A synthetic creation, a man-made gem,
Technetium, the element, a priceless gem.

In medicine's embrace, it finds its call,
A tracer of life, a savior for all.
Through veins it courses, a diagnostic ray,
Revealing diseases, keeping darkness at bay.

In industry's grasp, it fuels the way,
Catalyst of progress, where miracles sway.

From oil refineries to nuclear might,
Technetium, the element, a guiding light.
    Its radioactive dance, a mesmerizing chore,
Unleashing energy, forevermore.
A testament to human endeavor,
Exploring the unknown, with courage to endeavor.
    Technetium, a symbol of hope,
A catalyst for progress, our horizons to elope.
In laboratories, its mysteries unfold,
Unraveling the universe, with stories yet untold.
    Oh, Technetium, element divine,
In your atomic structure, wonders align.
A testament to human mind's finesse,
Unlocking the secrets, with scientific progress.
    So let us celebrate, with joy and cheer,
Technetium, the element, forever held dear.
For in your essence, we find our way,
A beacon of knowledge, guiding us each day.

NINETEEN

NO NORTH

In the realm of science, a jewel does gleam,
A radiant element, Technetium its name.
With atomic number 43, it takes its place,
A symbol of progress, a beacon of grace.

In the depths of the cosmos, where stars ignite,
Technetium shines, casting its ethereal light.
A catalyst for discovery, unlocking the unknown,
Revealing the secrets the universe has sown.

In medicine's embrace, it finds its worth,
A tool for diagnosis, a gift to unearth.
Through nuclear imaging, it unveils the unseen,
Guiding doctors' hands with precision so keen.

Radiating energy, it dances with might,
A radioactive element, a wonder in sight.

Its isotopes decay, emitting a glow,
A testament to nature's ebb and flow.

In industry's embrace, it aids in creation,
Catalyzing reactions, a symbol of innovation.
From catalysts to superalloys, it plays a role,
Aiding in progress, a mission to extol.

Technetium, oh element, shining so bright,
A symbol of hope, a beacon of light.
In science and medicine, you pave the way,
Unveiling the mysteries, each and every day.

So let us celebrate, this element divine,
Technetium, the jewel of science, so fine.
With boundless potential, it leads us forth,
Into a future where progress has no north.

TWENTY

INCREDIBLE POWER

In the realm of atoms, a hidden treasure lies,
A metal, a marvel, that defies the skies.
Technetium, the element of endless worth,
Unveils the secrets hidden beneath the Earth.

Radiant and rare, it dances with delight,
A symbol of progress, shining so bright.
In medical imaging, it takes center stage,
Guiding doctors' hands, turning the page.

A beacon of hope, in the darkest hour,
Technetium's power, an incredible power.
Diagnosis, its mission, unlocking the gate,
Revealing the truth, determining fate.

With gamma rays, it peers into our souls,
Unveiling mysteries, making us whole.

From heart to bone, it paints a vivid scene,
A lifeline of clarity, where answers convene.
    In labs and reactors, its story unfolds,
Fueling innovation, as new tales are told.
An element of progress, a catalyst for change,
Technetium, forever we rearrange.
    From factories to fields, it lights up the way,
A testament to human endeavor, we say.
For in its existence, a promise resides,
To push boundaries, where science collides.
    Technetium, oh element divine,
A symbol of hope, where wonders intertwine.
With each discovery, a step towards the sublime,
A tribute to the triumph of mankind.

TWENTY-ONE

FOREVER TRUE

In the realm of science, a luminary shines,
A hidden gem, Technetium, its brilliance defines.
A symbol of progress, discovery's delight,
Unveiling truths, casting shadows to ignite.

In the depths of atoms, its story unfolds,
A testament to human endeavor, untold.
A beacon of hope, guiding us through,
Technetium, oh how we depend on you.

In the realm of medicine, you take center stage,
A diagnostic tool, a healer's sage.
Through gamma rays, you illuminate,
The inner workings of our fragile state.

From heart to bones, you unveil the unknown,
Aiding doctors, their knowledge grown.
With radioactive embrace, you reveal,
The secrets within, our bodies, you heal.

In the realm of industry, you play a key role,
A catalyst for progress, a vital soul.
From nuclear power to industrial might,
Technetium, you're an illuminating light.

In laboratories, your presence is felt,
Unraveling mysteries, where others have dwelt.
A trailblazer, forging paths anew,
Technetium, we owe it all to you.

So let us celebrate this element rare,
Technetium, a symbol of knowledge we share.
With every discovery, every breakthrough,
We honor your essence, forever true.

TWENTY-TWO

SCIENCE WE PROCLAIM

In medicine's realm, an element dwells,
A marvel of science, where healing compels.
Technetium, thy name, a beacon of light,
Guiding us through darkness, unveiling the night.

With gamma rays dancing, it reveals the way,
Diagnosing ailments, where answers may stray.
Injected with care, it courses through veins,
Mapping out mysteries, relieving our pains.

In industry's embrace, you find your worth,
A catalyst, transforming the Earth.
From refineries to oil fields afar,
Technetium's touch, a shining star.

But amidst your brilliance, a secret you hide,
A radioactive nature, impossible to chide.

Half-lives and isotopes, a dance with decay,
Scientific progress, forging the way.

From laboratories to reactors of might,
Technetium's power, a captivating sight.
Unraveling atoms, unlocking the key,
To knowledge and progress, for you and for me.

Oh Technetium, symbol of human endeavor,
In your essence, mysteries we uncover.
Through diagnostics and industry's strive,
Your legacy, forever alive.

So let us hail Technetium's grand delight,
A symbol of knowledge, a beacon of light.
With each discovery, we celebrate your name,
Technetium, forever, in science we proclaim.

TWENTY-THREE

COSMIC BAZAARS

In the realm of medicine, a secret lies,
A metal of wonder, that time defies.
Technetium, oh element divine,
A beacon of hope, a treasure we find.

    Radiant and rare, a gift from the stars,
With gamma rays dancing in cosmic bazaars.
In nuclear hearts, its story unfolds,
Unveiling the mysteries that science beholds.

    A tracer in veins, it whispers the truth,
Revealing the path of illness, resolute.
From brain to bone, its journey takes flight,
Guiding the healers, igniting the light.

    Imaging machines, with Technetium's aid,
Peering inside, where shadows pervade.

Tumors and fractures, they tremble and fade,
As hope springs forth in this metal cascade.
    A warrior element, mighty and strong,
Unleashing its power, where progress belongs.
A symbol of science, innovation's crest,
Technetium, the element, we are truly blessed.

TWENTY-FOUR

WONDERS OF ETERNITY

In the realm of industry, where wonders unfold,
A metal emerged, a tale yet untold.
Technetium, the element of might,
A catalyst for progress, shining bright.

Born in the stars, a cosmic affair,
Within its nucleus, secrets it does bear.
Unstable and rare, it dances with glee,
Radiating energy, setting atoms free.

In factories it toils, a worker unseen,
Igniting reactions, creating routines.
From metal alloys to glowing glass,
Technetium weaves its transformative mass.

In power plants, it whispers with might,
Fueling the core, a nuclear light.

Its isotopes dance, a fiery waltz,
Harnessing energy, untamed and false.
 But beyond the realms of industry and might,
Technetium unveils a wondrous sight.
In medicine's hands, it finds a new role,
A beacon of hope, a diagnostic stroll.
 Injected with care, into veins it flows,
Mapping the body, revealing its throes.
A tracer of life, it guides the way,
Unveiling mysteries, night and day.
 Technetium, oh element divine,
A symbol of progress, forever to shine.
From industry's grasp to science's embrace,
You illuminate the unknown, with grace.
 So let us celebrate, this element rare,
Technetium, the answer to our prayer.
For in its existence, we find a key,
To unlock the wonders of eternity.

TWENTY-FIVE

UNLOCKING THE FUTURE

In the realm of science, a star does gleam,
A radiant element, Technetium by name.
With atomic number forty-three, it claims,
A place on the periodic table's grand frame.

In medicine, it holds a special role,
A tracer that illuminates, body and soul.
Injected with care, it journeys within,
Revealing secrets, where mysteries begin.

Through veins and arteries, it swiftly flows,
Mapping paths, where ailments impose.
Diagnostics aided, with precision and might,
Technetium shines, revealing the light.

In industry, it finds its own domain,
A catalyst, driving progress with no disdain.

In the realm of progress, it plays its part,
Transforming elements, with a masterful art.

A symbol of innovation, it stands tall,
Pushing boundaries, breaking down walls.
In laboratories, minds set ablaze,
Technetium's essence, a scientific maze.

Oh, Technetium, element so rare,
Your presence, a beacon, beyond compare.
In medicine and industry, you hold the key,
Unlocking the future, where wonders will be.

TWENTY-SIX

ANNALS OF SPACE

In the realm of doctors, a silent hero resides,
Technetium, the element that guides.
With gamma rays, it illuminates the way,
Unraveling mysteries, night and day.

Through medical diagnostics, it takes its flight,
Aiding physicians in their healing might.
Injected into veins, it seeks its course,
Revealing secrets with its radioactive force.

In the realm of industry, it plays its part,
Technetium, a symbol of progress, a piece of art.
From nuclear reactors to cutting-edge tech,
It pushes the boundaries, always on the trek.

Its isotopes dance with atoms in fusion,
Unleashing energy, a powerful illusion.

With its unique properties, it unlocks the door,
To a world of possibilities, forevermore.

Technetium, a beacon of knowledge and might,
A catalyst of innovation, shining bright.
In labs and hospitals, its story unfolds,
A testament to the wonders that science holds.

So let us celebrate this element with cheer,
For Technetium's discoveries are crystal clear.
A symbol of hope, progress, and unfound grace,
Forever it shall stand, in the annals of space.

TWENTY-SEVEN

ENLIGHTENING OUR MINDS

In the realm of atoms, a mystery unfolds,
A tale of Technetium, a story yet untold.
With atomic number 43, it shines bright,
A radiant element, filled with endless light.

In medical imaging, it takes the lead,
A beacon of hope, fulfilling a crucial need.
Injected into veins, it explores within,
Unraveling secrets, where diseases begin.

Radiopharmaceuticals, a miracle to behold,
Technetium's isotopes, they expertly mold.
They dance through the body, seeking their place,
Guided by science, with grace they embrace.

In industry, it plays a vital role,
A catalyst supreme, with a purpose to extol.

Oil refining, chemical reactions thrive,
Technetium, the catalyst, helps them survive.

Scientific progress owes much to this friend,
Its unique properties, a treasure to defend.
From nuclear reactors to space exploration,
Technetium's contribution, a source of elation.

So let us celebrate this element grand,
A testament to human knowledge, hand in hand.
Technetium, a symbol of our quest for more,
Enlightening our minds, forever to explore.

TWENTY-EIGHT

CURIOSITY'S ARC

In the realm of science, a marvel we behold,
A metal of mystery, shining bright and bold.
Technetium, the element, rare and unique,
Unveiling secrets, answers it seeks.

In laboratories, it dances with grace,
A catalyst for progress, in every place.
From medicine's grasp, it finds its way,
Unlocking the doors of healing, day by day.

Radiopharmaceuticals, its magical art,
Guiding us to the depths of the human heart.
With gamma rays, it reveals the unseen,
Diagnosing ailments, where hope has been.

In industry's embrace, it finds its worth,
Fuels the engines of innovation, giving birth.

To tools and devices that push us ahead,
Creating a future where dreams are fed.

 Oh, Technetium, a pioneer of light,
Guiding humanity through the darkest of night.
A beacon of knowledge, a flame in the dark,
Igniting the spark of curiosity's arc.

 From stars to labs, its journey unfolds,
A testament to human courage, untold.
Technetium, we salute your might,
A symbol of progress, shining so bright.

TWENTY-NINE

PIONEER OF PROGRESS

In the realm of elements, a hidden gem we find,
Technetium, a beacon of light, one of a kind.
With atomic number forty-three, it shines bright,
Unveiling secrets, pushing boundaries with its might.

In medicine's embrace, a hero it becomes,
A tracer of life, where hope hums.
Radiopharmaceuticals, its magical spell,
Guiding us through darkness, where mysteries dwell.

In industry's grasp, it fuels innovation's fire,
Catalyzing change, taking us higher.
From catalysts to high-temperature alloys,
Technetium, the key, unlocking industrial joys.

In scientific progress, it takes a leading role,
Transmuting elements, expanding knowledge's scroll.

Nuclear reactors, where energy thrives,
Technetium's magic, the power it derives.

    A symbol of hope, an enlightenment's guide,
Technetium, our ally, standing beside.
Unraveling the universe, expanding our sight,
A testament to human curiosity's might.

    Oh, Technetium, you shine through the dark,
A pioneer of progress, leaving your mark.
With every discovery, a new chapter we write,
In the tapestry of science, your brilliance takes flight.

    So, let us celebrate this element divine,
Technetium, the spark that makes us shine.
Innovation's companion, knowledge's key,
Forever inspiring our quest to be free.

THIRTY

ABUNDANT AND STRONG

In the realm of diagnostics, it shines bright,
A beacon of hope, a guiding light.
Technetium, the element of wonder,
Unveiling secrets, tearing veils asunder.

Within the realm of medicine, it dwells,
A healer in disguise, a cure that compels.
Through gamma rays, it reveals the unseen,
Aiding doctors, unraveling the unseen.

From radiopharmaceuticals, it takes its form,
Injecting life into veins, a medical norm.
For scans and tests, it plays its part,
Guiding the way, a diagnostic art.

But Technetium's role does not end there,
In industry, it finds a purpose to share.

Catalysts and superconductors, it creates,
Driving progress, opening new gates.

In nuclear reactors, it finds its place,
A fuel that powers, with atomic grace.
Its isotopes, abundant and strong,
Fulfilling energy needs, all day long.

With unique properties, it does impress,
A low melting point, a metal to possess.
Its radioactive nature, a scientific boon,
Unraveling mysteries, like the light of the moon.

Technetium, symbol of progress and light,
A catalyst of knowledge, shining bright.
In labs and industries, it plays its role,
Revealing the unseen, a gift to behold.

THIRTY-ONE

ENDLESS DELIGHT

In the realm of elements, a gem does shine,
Technetium, the name that's so divine.
A wondrous metal, rare and pure,
Unraveling secrets, it does endure.

In the heart of industry, it finds its place,
Catalyzing reactions with elegant grace.
A catalyst supreme, it sparks innovation,
Driving progress with its potent creation.

Within nuclear reactors, it takes its form,
A fuel that powers, beautifully warm.
Unleashing energy, a mighty force,
Technetium, a gift, from nature's course.

Its properties unique, a marvel to behold,
Unraveling mysteries, untold.

A beacon of knowledge, a guiding light,
Technetium, shining ever so bright.
   Symbol of progress, symbol of might,
Unleashing wonders, day and night.
A symbol of freedom, in the pursuit of truth,
Technetium, a gem of eternal youth.
   Oh Technetium, we celebrate your name,
Innovation and science, forever you claim.
With every discovery, we honor your might,
Technetium, a symbol, of endless delight.

THIRTY-TWO

HIGHER AND HIGHER

In the realm of science and innovation,
There lies a metal with a noble mission.
Technetium, a symbol of progress and might,
Shining bright in the corridors of scientific light.

A catalyst it is, with powers unseen,
Igniting reactions, like a spark serene.
In industry's embrace, it finds its rightful place,
Aiding transformations with an elegant grace.

With unique properties that set it apart,
Technetium unveils its wondrous art.
Radiation dances, a symphony so grand,
Aiding medical diagnostics, a healing hand.

Through gamma rays, it peeks into our core,
Unveiling secrets, hidden forevermore.

A beacon of knowledge, it guides the way,
In the realm of medicine, a vital display.
 Scientific progress owes much to its name,
Technetium, a catalyst for fortune and fame.
In industry, a fuel for innovation's fire,
A symbol of progress, soaring higher and higher.
 Oh, Technetium, element of wonder and might,
A guiding star in the darkest night.
Through your power and grace, we are inspired,
To reach for new frontiers, with hearts untired.

THIRTY-THREE

INSPIRE AND GUIDE

Technetium, catalyst of creation,
A shimmering light in the realm of science.
With atomic number 43, you stand tall,
A symbol of progress, knowledge, and defiance.

In reactions, you play a vital role,
A catalyst, igniting the flame of change.
Transforming elements, forging new paths,
In the alchemy of nature, you rearrange.

From the depths of stars, you were born,
In stellar explosions, your genesis unfolded.
A cosmic dance, a celestial symphony,
Your atoms scattered, destiny yet molded.

In labs, your secrets we unravel,
Unveiling mysteries, hidden in your core.
Medical diagnostics, a realm you conquer,
Revealing truths, never seen before.

Innovation, industry, you fuel the fire,
With nuclear power, you pave the way.
A source of energy, limitless and bold,
You drive progress, day by day.

Technetium, you inspire and guide,
A beacon of hope, in the quest for more.
In science, medicine, and human endeavor,
You shine bright, forever at the core.

THIRTY-FOUR

CREATOR OF ART

In the realm of elements, a star is born,
Technetium, a jewel, rare and unknown.
With atomic number forty-three,
It dances with electrons, wild and free.

A catalyst it is, in industry's embrace,
Unraveling mysteries, with its glowing grace.
In medical diagnostics, it finds its place,
A beacon of hope, a healer's embrace.

Its radioactive nature, a force to behold,
Unveiling the unseen, its story unfolds.
A fuel for innovation, progress it ignites,
Unleashing the power of scientific lights.

From labs to reactors, it plays its part,
A silent hero, a creator of art.

A glimpse into the depths of the unknown,
Technetium, a guide, a pathway shown.
  With power and grace, it lights the way,
Inspiring minds, like a sun's bright ray.
Oh Technetium, a symbol of might,
Forever shining, in science's light.

THIRTY-FIVE

TECHNETIUM, ELEMENT OF MYSTERY

In nuclear reactors, you hold great might,
Technetium, element of the night.
With a half-life short, you dance and decay,
Radiating energy, lighting the way.

    A synthetic wonder, born in a lab,
Your isotopes glow, a nuclear cab.
Unstable and rare, you defy the norm,
A mystery element, in science you form.

    In industry's grasp, you find your place,
Driving progress with your atomic embrace.
Catalyst of change, you speed up the game,
Creating new materials, with infinite aim.

In steel alloys, you lend strength and might,
Resisting corrosion, shining so bright.
Your magnetic properties, a gift so pure,
Transforming technology, forever endure.

In medical diagnostics, you take the stage,
A tracer of life, revealing the page.
From bone scans to tumors, you guide the way,
Helping doctors detect, day after day.

From stellar explosions, you were once born,
A cosmic creation, in brilliance adorned.
Now in human hands, your power we wield,
In science, in industry, your wonders revealed.

Technetium, element of mystery and might,
Forever shining, in the realms of light.

ABOUT THE AUTHOR

Walter the Educator is one of the pseudonyms for Walter Anderson. Formally educated in Chemistry, Business, and Education, he is an educator, an author, a diverse entrepreneur, and he is the son of a disabled war veteran. "Walter the Educator" shares his time between educating and creating. He holds interests and owns several creative projects that entertain, enlighten, enhance, and educate, hoping to inspire and motivate you.

Follow, find new works, and stay up to date
with Walter the Educator™
at WaltertheEducator.com

www.ingramcontent.com/pod-product-compliance
Lightning Source LLC
LaVergne TN
LVHW052000060526
838201LV00059B/3745